About the Author

Deepak Chopra is one of the world's greatest leaders in the field of mind/body medicine. He is a *New York Times* bestselling author of both non-fiction and fiction. His books have been translated into over thirty-five languages including *Ageless Body, Timeless Mind*.

Visit him at deepakchopra.com

ALSO BY DEEPAK CHOPRA

THE
ULTIMATE
HAPPINESS
PRESCRIPTION

7 Keys to Joy and Enlightenment

DEEPAK CHOPRA

RIDER

LONDON · SYDNEY · AUCKLAND · JOHANNESBURG

1 3 5 7 9 10 8 6 4 2

First published in the UK in 2010 by Rider, an imprint of Ebury Publishing.
This edition published in 2017

First published in the USA by Harmony Books, an imprint of the Crown
Publishing Group, in 2009

Ebury Publishing is a Random House Group company

Copyright © 2009 by Deepak Chopra

Deepak Chopra has asserted his right to be identified as the author of this work
in accordance with the Copyright, Designs and Patents Act 1988.

All rights reserved. No part of this publication may be reproduced, stored in a
retrieval system, or transmitted in any form or by any means, electronic,
mechanical, photocopying, recording or otherwise, without the prior permission
of the copyright owner.

The Random House Group Limited Reg. No. 954009

Addresses for companies within the Random House Group can be found at
www.rbooks.co.uk

A CIP catalogue record for this book is available from the British Library

The Random House Group Limited supports The Forest Stewardship
Council (FSC), the leading international forest certification organisation.
All our titles that are printed on Greenpeace approved FSC certified paper
carry the FSC logo. Our paper procurement policy can be found at
www.rbooks.co.uk/environment

Printed in the UK by Clays Ltd, St Ives PLC

Design by Maria Elias

ISBN 9781846042386

Copies are available at special rates for bulk orders. Contact the sales
development team on 020 7840 8487 for more information.

To buy books by your favourite authors and register for offers, visit
www.rbooks.co.uk

To the happiness that heals.

Contents

The Ultimate Happiness

The purpose of life is the expansion of happiness. Happiness is the goal of every other goal. Most people are under the impression that happiness comes from becoming successful, accumulating wealth, being healthy, and having good relationships. There is certainly enormous social pressure to believe that these accomplishments are the same as achieving happiness. However, this is a mistake. Success, wealth, good health, and nurturing relationships are *byproducts* of happiness, not the cause.

When you are happy, you are more likely to make choices that lead to all these things. The reverse isn't true. Everyone has observed people who are deeply unhappy even after they have attained incredible wealth and success. Good health can be taken for granted and abused. And even the happiest family can find its happiness ruined by a sudden crisis. Unhappy people are not successful, and no amount of money and achievement will change the equation.

So let's shift our gaze beyond external indications to inner happiness, which we all want to attain and yet which remains elusive. In the last few years psychologists and brain researchers have undertaken the first serious research on happiness. Previously, the field of psychology was almost entirely focused on treating unhappiness, much the way internal medicine is based on treating disease. But just as interest in wellness and prevention has dramatically risen in recent years, so has interest in happiness.

Surprisingly, one of the most controversial topics in this new field of positive psychology is whether human beings are actually meant to be happy. Perhaps we are all pursuing an illusion, a fantasy fueled by occasional moments of happiness that can never turn into a permanent state. Or perhaps some people are genetically predisposed to be happy, and they will be the lucky few who escape what the rest of us experience, which is a kind of low-level contentment at best. Some experts contend that happiness occurs by chance, an emotional surprise that quickly comes and goes, like a surprise birthday party, leaving no permanent change once the event is over.

Leading researchers in the new field of positive psychology, in particular professors Sonja Lyubomirsky, Ed Diener, and Martin Seligman, came up with what they call the happiness formula. These researchers found three specific factors that could be quantified in a simple equation:

THE ULTIMATE HAPPINESS PRESCRIPTION

$$H = S + C + V$$

OR

HAPPINESS = SET POINT + CONDITIONS OF LIVING
+ VOLUNTARY ACTIVITIES

Since this is one of the leading theories of happiness, we'll explore it before showing that there is a better way to reach the goal. Although it helps point the way, the happiness formula doesn't go deep enough to uncover the real secret of happiness.

The first factor, S, is the brain's set point, which determines how naturally happy you are. Unhappy people have a brain mechanism that interprets situations as problems. Happy people, on the other hand, have a brain mechanism that interprets the very same situations as opportunities. So the "glass half full, glass half empty" phenomenon is rooted in the brain, and is "set" in a way that doesn't vary much over time. According to the researchers, a person's set point is responsible for something like 40 percent of the experience of happiness. Apparently, this set point is partly genetic. If your parents were unhappy, you have a higher likelihood of being unhappy as well. But there are also childhood influences to take into account.

Children's brains have neurons that mirror the brains of

adults in their surroundings. These so-called mirror neurons are responsible for the way children learn new behaviors, so the theory goes. As they develop, young children don't have to imitate their parents in order to learn something new; they only have to observe them, and certain brain cells will fire in a way that mirrors the activity. For example, a baby being weaned from breast-feeding watches how her parents eat. As they reach for food and put it into their mouths, certain areas of their brains light up. Simply watching this activity leads the same areas to light up in the infant's brain. In this way the newly forming infant brain learns a new behavior without ever having to go through trial and error alone.

This model has already been tested in monkeys and theoretically extended to humans. It provides a physical explanation for something as mysterious as empathy, the ability to feel what someone else is feeling. Some people have this ability; others don't. A few saintly individuals have so much empathy that they can hardly bear it when someone else is suffering. Research with MRIs and CAT scans suggests that brain function plays a major role in empathy. A child's neurons mirror the emotions of adults around him, leading the child to actually feel what his parents feel. So if a youngster is surrounded by unhappy adults, his nervous system will be programmed for unhappiness, even before he has any cause for unhappiness himself.

Why doesn't every child learn empathy? Because brain development is wildly complex and never the same for two babies. When we were infants, all kinds of brain functions were being programmed at the same time, and for some of us, empathy was only assigned a minor role. This is a troubling inequality, and it extends to happiness. When you see the brain has a set point for happiness, traceable either to genetics or childhood influences, it's all too easy to conclude that nothing can be done about it. However, this would be a mistake, because neither the brain nor your genes are fixed structures; instead, they are in process every minute of your life, constantly changing and evolving. You are still being influenced at the genetic level by new experiences. Every choice you make sends chemical signals coursing through your brain, including the choice to be happy, and each signal helps to shape the brain from year to year.

In the overall picture, research has shown that the brain's set point can be changed by the following:

Drugs that act as mood elevators, which work only in the short term and have side effects.

Cognitive therapy, which changes the brain by helping us change our limiting beliefs. We all tell ourselves stories in our heads that provoke unhappiness. Repeating the same negative belief over and over ("I am a victim," "I am unloved," "Life isn't fair, something's wrong with me," etc.) creates neural pathways that reinforce negativity by turning it into a habitual way of thinking. Such beliefs can be replaced with others that are not simply more positive, but are a better match with reality (I may have been a victim in the past but I don't have to remain that way; I can find love if I choose better places to look for it, etc.). In treating patients whose lives are dominated by negative beliefs, psychologists have found that altering really fundamental beliefs can be as effective in changing brain chemistry as prescribing drugs.

Meditation, which alters the brain in many positive ways. The physical effects of sitting quietly and going inward are amazingly extensive. It took a long time to unravel the puzzle. Researchers had to work against the Western assumption that meditation was mystical or at best a kind of religious practice. Now we realize that it activates the prefrontal cortex—the seat of higher thinking—and stimulates the release of neurotransmitters, including dopamine, serotonin, oxytocin, and brain opiates. Each of these naturally occurring brain chemicals has been linked to different aspects of happiness. Dopamine is an antidepressant; serotonin is associated with increased self-esteem; oxytocin is now believed to be the pleasure hormone (its levels also elevate during sexual arousal); opiates are the body's painkillers, which also provide the exhilaration associated with runner's high. It should be obvious, then, that meditation, by creating higher levels of these neurotransmitters, is a more effective way of changing the brain's set point for happiness. No single drug can simultaneously choreograph the coordinated release of all these chemicals.

The second factor in the happiness formula is *C*, or conditions of living. Because we all want to improve our quality of life, we take it for granted that moving from bad conditions to good ones will make us happier. But apparently this factor accounts for only 7 to 12 percent of the total happiness experience. If you win the lottery, for example, at first you will be ecstatically happy. But by the end of one year you will have returned to your baseline level of happiness or unhappiness. After five years almost all lottery winners report that the experience has actually made their lives worse. Experts on stress have coined the term "eustress," to describe the stress caused by intensely pleasurable experiences. We all think we'd like to experience this, yet the body cannot tell the difference between eustress and distress. Either one can trigger the stress reaction. If you don't adapt well to stress, good experiences can be just as taxing as bad ones to your heart, endocrine system, and other vital organs and systems.

Much like happy events, tragic circumstances, such as a death in the family, a bitter divorce, or a catastrophe such as becoming totally paralyzed after a spinal injury, do not significantly influence a person's level of happiness in the long term. People have a remarkable ability to adapt to outer circumstances. As Darwin said, the most important factor in survival is neither intelligence nor strength but adaptability. Emotional resilience, the ability to bounce back after something bad happens, is also one of the strongest indicators for who will live to be one hundred. Bad things happen to everyone, but being able to adapt afterward is a valuable trait that we come by naturally. Our remarkable ability to adapt explains why living conditions score so low as indicators of overall happiness.

Almost 50 percent of the happiness formula depends on the third factor, V, or voluntary activities—the things we choose to do every day. What kind of choice makes us happy? One kind is based on personal pleasure, but surprisingly, researchers did not find that these were the most significant. Increasing your personal pleasure by eating a good meal, drinking champagne, having sex, going to a movie, and so on will bring a temporary kind of happiness, for a few hours or at most a day or two. Instant gratification is followed by rapid fall-off.

Another kind of choice promotes creative expression or the happiness of another person. In both cases a deeper level of the self is being accessed. According to researchers, making other people happy proves to be a fast track to happiness, and its effect is long lasting. Turning to creative expression to make yourself happy can also generate positive results that last a lifetime.

This, in a nutshell, is what current research tells us. However, knowing the happiness formula doesn't guarantee true or lasting happiness. Only the third factor, V, reaches into the inner life of a person, opening the door to the only place where I believe we can truly find the secret of happiness. Let's see what lies beyond the door. What we find will also answer the most important question: Are humans capable of being truly, lastingly happy?

Eastern wisdom traditions point out that life inevitably contains suffering, which comes in many forms, including accidents, misfortune, aging, illness, and death. This implies that the pessimists are right when they claim that lasting happiness is an illusion. Human beings in particular suffer as the result of memory and imagination. We carry inside us the wounds of the past and imagine that the future will bring more pain. Other creatures are not burdened by worry over old age, decrepitude, and death. They don't hold on to the past, nursing grievances and resentment.

Animals do have memory. If you kick a dog, it will remember the experience and may snarl at you if it encounters you ten years later. But unlike a human being, a kicked dog won't plan for ten years how to get even. Our capacity to suffer makes us seek a way out. Therefore, for millions of people, today is planned around escaping yesterday's pain and avoiding pain tomorrow.

Instead of trying to escape suffering, Eastern wisdom traditions set about diagnosing suffering the way a physician diagnoses disease. In the Vedic and Buddhist traditions of ancient India, five main causes were linked to suffering and the unhappiness it causes.

1. Not knowing your true identity
2. Clinging to the idea of permanence in a world that is inherently impermanent

3. Fear of change
4. Identifying with the socially induced hallucination called the ego
5. Fear of death

Life has changed tremendously over the centuries, but these sources of suffering have not, so until we solve them, even the most powerful drugs, the most loving upbringing, and the most selfless efforts to make others happy won't really work. The happiness formula doesn't address the real ills of human existence, which we all experience. To be alive is to fear change, cling to the ego and its false promises, and fear the arrival of death. We ponder in confusion the most simple, basic question: *Who am I?*

Fortunately, it isn't necessary to wrestle with five causes of suffering. They are all contained in the first: ignorance of your true identity. Once you experience who you really are, all suffering will come to an end. This is, of course, a huge promise, but it has endured for at least three thousand years, waiting for each new generation to discover it. Every discovery is new and depends on the individual. By nature we are all interested in ourselves. If you take that interest and go deep inside, you can each find the place where your true self resides, and then the secret of happiness will unfold.

Your true identity lies in a core consciousness beyond the mind, intellect, and ego. When you look beyond your limited self—the "I" that struggles to find peace, love, and fulfillment in life—you are on the path to your true identity. We are all connected to the source of creation. Ancient sages have left us a beautiful image for this: a shrine in the heart that hides a small candle whose flame is eternal. When you have found that flame, you have found enlightenment, and then the darkness of doubt, anger, fear, and ignorance are dispelled.

Who you are transcends space, time, and cause-and-effect. Your core consciousness is immortal. If you know yourself at this level, you will never suffer again. Many people equate enlightenment with detachment, a remote state of isolation that seems frightening, because they assume that the comforts of everyday life must be sacrificed. If forced to choose between enlightenment and personal pleasure, they will always choose the latter. But knowing your true identity doesn't isolate you or detach you from the fulfillment of everyday life. On the contrary, this is where you discover the wellspring of all fulfillment.

At the source we discover a connection that binds us all. The real you is transpersonal, meaning that it extends beyond the boundaries of your personal self. *Transpersonal* doesn't mean "impersonal," however, which is another thing people fear when they think of enlightenment. Once again, the opposite is true. As an inspiring Indian spiritual teacher once put it, "My love radiates like light from a bonfire. It is focused on none and denied to none." If you value love, peace, and fulfillment, finding your true identity expands those things manyfold.

Fortunately, knowing your real self is not difficult. It's what nature intended for us. Once you find the path, one step follows the next without stress and strain. A small grain of trust is needed at the beginning. In Western society few of us are raised to believe that the only permanent cure for unhappiness is enlightenment, but you can experience the truth of this yourself. Even the early steps on the path remove some suffering, often dramatically.

From where you sit at this moment, reading this page, enlightenment may sound like a daunting and remote prospect, but in the following pages I will provide seven keys to guide you on your journey. Since what works best is always simple, natural, and effortless, let me offer you a single idea that is tremendously powerful.

In the world of constant change, there is something that doesn't change.

This simple thought describes the goal of all seeking. If

you focus on your breath, you can feel it rise and fall. If you focus on your thoughts, you can observe them come and go as well. Every function in your body ebbs and flows, and in fact, the whole world works the same way.

Where does this waxing and waning come from? Where is the nonchange that makes change possible? It must exist. Without the calm ocean, you couldn't have waves. Without a quiet mind, you couldn't have thoughts. Without a so-called ground state, a domain of infinite potential for matter and energy, physics tells us that there could be no universe.

Observing that all change is based on nonchange is tremendously important. It points up that your existence, which is enmeshed in change, must be rooted in a deeper state of being that never changes. You have a source, the ground state. Think of anything you can observe—a tree, a sunset, the moon at night, or a distant star. You, the observer, and the thing you observe will one day pass away. Both are caught up in impermanence. But the underlying ground state doesn't come and go; it remains the same.

Enlightenment simply consists of finding a way to reach this ground state. Having found it, you naturally identify with it. You are able to say, "This is the true me." That's all there is to enlightenment, which means the secret to happiness is in your hands. The seven keys to happiness could also be called the seven keys to enlightenment. They consist of simple, everyday things to consider and do. No drastic change in lifestyle is required. You don't have to tell anyone else that you are on the path to enlightenment. But others will observe that you are becoming happier and more fulfilled.

The process that leads to enlightenment is gradual and requires patience, but fortunately the very act of seeking it yields fruit right here and now. Any step you take toward your core consciousness—your ground state, your true self—obliterates some causes of unhappiness in your life. At the same time, the innate happiness that is your birthright will blossom. Thus you are on a twofold path: to eliminate darkness and to bring on the light.

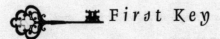 First Key

BE AWARE
OF YOUR BODY

Your body and the universe are a single field
of energy, information, and consciousness.
The body is your connection to the cosmic
computer, which is organizing an infinity of
events simultaneously. By listening to your
body and responding to it with awareness,
you tap into the field of infinite possibility,
where the natural experience is peace,
harmony, and joy.

There is but one temple in the universe . . . and
that is the human body.

—Thomas Carlyle

Your first and most reliable guide to happiness is your body. The body is designed to support the mind, and working together they create the state known as happiness. When you're deciding whether or not to act, ask your body, "How do you feel about this?" If your body sends back a signal of physical or emotional distress, reconsider the action. If your body sends a signal of comfort and eagerness, proceed. Together, mind and body form a single field. It is artificial to separate them as we usually do. Every experience has a physical component. If you're hungry, the mind and stomach are hungry together. If you have an incredible spiritual experience, your heart and liver cells share in it. You cannot have a single thought, sensation, or feeling without your body responding.

The first key to happiness tells us that by being aware of your body, you are connecting to the underlying field of infinite possibilities. Why do mind, body, and spirit feel separate when they are not? Because of lack of awareness. Awareness has tremendous power. It tunes into every cell. It regulates the body's countless interactions. Awareness is the invisible, silent agent that lets your body know what your mind is thinking, and at the same time it sends feedback from the body so that the mind feels supported and understood. Ideally, when you experience being loved, your mind will grasp that you are loved, your cells will be nourished by that love, and your soul will rejoice that you have reached deep enough to find the source of love. Every good thing in life saturates your whole being.

When mind, body, and spirit are in harmony, happiness is the natural result. Signs of the absence of harmony, on the other hand, are discomfort, pain, depression, anxiety, and illness in general. Unhappiness is a form of feedback. It signals that disharmony has entered the field somewhere— either in mind, body, or spirit. Awareness has become disconnected. Only when we look at the situation in this holistic way can we link health, wholeness, and holiness, for all three share the same root word, and all three share the same state of harmony or disharmony. You may have heard the saying "The issues are in the tissues." This refers to the fact that psychological issues such as anger, depression, neurosis, hostility, and free-floating anxiety are not simply psychological. They have a correlate in the brain, and through the central nervous system the brain makes every cell and tissue in your body aware that you have an issue.

The entire field quivers at the slightest twinge of pain or pleasure. In other words, the field is aware. When you consciously pay attention to what your body is telling you, this awareness is tremendously increased. Awareness isn't the same as having a thought. A mother is aware of how her child feels without having to think "A is bothering him" or "B has gone wrong." Awareness is intuitive. All you have to do is pay attention, and awareness grants you access to every corner of the infinite field. This is like being plugged into the cosmic computer, because when the field organizes the smallest thing in creation, it organizes the whole.

The opposite is also true. When you withdraw awareness, disruptions occur on many levels at the same time. Feedback loops no longer operate as they should between mind and body. The flow of energy and nourishment needed by every cell begins to diminish. By not paying attention to your body, you are putting it in the same predicament as a neglected child. How can a child be expected to develop normally if the parents pay no attention, if they ignore its cries for help, and remain indifferent to whether their child is happy or unhappy? The same question applies to the body, and it leads to the same answer. The body doesn't stop developing around age twenty, an arbitrary time we call maturity. Constant change is always taking place, all the way down to the level of genes. Change is never neutral. Either it leads to growth, development, and evolution or it leads in the opposite direction, toward decline, decay, and disorder. The difference depends on how you pay attention, because attention is your connection to the field of infinite possibilities.

The field has certain qualities or attributes that support mind, body, and spirit. There are three qualities that contribute to happiness most significantly. Intelligence is the first. When you listen to your body, you eavesdrop on the mind of the universe. This involves many tasks at once. A human body can think thoughts, play a piano, secrete hormones, regulate skin temperature, kill germs, remove toxins, and make a baby all at the same time. That is a miraculous display of intelligence. This intelligence also allows you to make choices that lead to fulfillment.

Fulfillment seems mysterious to many people, but we can break it down into its simplest parts. Fulfillment is the result of right thought, right feelings, and right action. Each area involves the body. We don't have to create artificial boundaries between a liver cell that makes a right choice and the mind making a right choice. Intelligence embraces both. If it makes a mistake at the chemical or genetic level, the cell dies or becomes malignant. The mind discriminates right from wrong at a different level, the level of ethics and morals. The emotions have their own level, discriminating between nourishing and toxic feelings, or between loving and harmful relationships. When you are consciously aware of your body and what it is telling you, the quality of intelligence is amplified. Its reach is infinite. While the human body performs countless physical processes, it tracks the movement of stars and planets, because your biological rhythms are actually the symphony of the whole universe. That's why we call it the universe—"one verse," "one song."

The second attribute of the field is creativity. Creativity keeps the flow of life fresh and new. It prevents inertia; it dispels habit. Much of the time the body seems stuck in routine. One breath is the same as another, one heartbeat repeats the action that came before. Simply to process food and air, your cells must endlessly repeat the same chemical processes with tremendous accuracy; no improvisation is allowed. But miraculously, the body also has complete flexibility to adapt to new situations. When you decide to do something new—have a baby, run a marathon, or climb a mountain—billions of cells adapt to your intention. This flexibility isn't mechanical. It's not like your car accelerating because you push down on the gas pedal. Rather, your body adapts creatively.

You can observe this in how creatively you can think and speak. No two thoughts are required to be exactly alike; no two sentences demand exactly the same words. The brain displays a pattern of neural activity to match any thought or sentence, even if that thought or sentence has never before appeared in the history of the universe. The ancient Vedic wisdom tradition in India identified creativity with *Ananda,* or bliss. Bliss is usually described as intense joy, but cells have their own bliss in the form of vitality, flow, and infinite dynamism.

To be most alive is to be in bliss. When you are in that state, everything feels possible. Your body is no longer a burden; you feel light as air. Nothing is old or stale. Instead, your creative potential is ignited. Creativity depends on the constant ability of life to refresh itself, and that ability is founded on bliss. You don't have to force yourself to be blissful—you couldn't if you tried—but only to be aware. Bliss is innate in awareness, which by its nature is lively, alert, effervescent, and joyful. The absence of those things can be corrected simply by accessing deeper awareness.

The third attribute of the field is power. Although cells operate on a microscopic level, they contain the power to survive, thrive, and evolve in an environment that erodes entire mountain ranges and dries up vast ancient seas. Power doesn't mean aggression. The power you don't see or feel is the greatest power of all. It organizes a thousand billion cells into one smoothly operating organism. It defends against every virus and germ that could harm the body, and monitors outbreaks of cancer inside the body itself.

Once again, it is entirely artificial to put boundaries around this quality of the field. Mind, body, and spirit express power in their own ways. The mind expresses power as attention and intention, turning wisps of thought into outward achievement. The body expresses power through physical strength and endurance, but also by organizing infinite processes into a coherent whole. Spirit expresses power by turning pure potential into reality. In the Indian tradition, spiritual power, called Shakti, is the most fundamental. When you possess Shakti, you can turn the invisible into the visible. Whatever you imagine manifests as reality. There are no obstacles between your desire and its fulfillment.

Shakti isn't mystical. It's an innate quality of awareness, without which invisible molecules of oxygen would drift randomly through the atmosphere. Apply awareness, and those same molecules carry life to every cell in the body. Going even deeper, Shakti allows you to cocreate the universe. You are not a passive observer in the cosmos. The entire universe is expressing itself through you at this very minute. It knows itself through you as awareness folds back on itself. Like a transformer that steps down the massive voltage running through high-tension power lines, your body steps down the energy of the universe to human scale. But it remains the same power. The infinitesimal electric charge emitted by a single brain cell is exactly the same as the firestorm of electromagnetism in an entire galaxy. This power is channeled through awareness, which means that when you become aware of anything, inside or outside yourself, you are increasing your share of power in the universe.

I want you to see that this one simple act—being aware of your body—unleashes intelligence, creativity, and power. Being aware isn't trivial, and it isn't optional, either. Once you withdraw your awareness by being distracted, depressed, restless, unhappy, or anxious, the flow of intelligence, creativity, and power is broken off. Most of the "natural" decay and disease seen in old age is actually the unnatural outcome of decreased awareness, which is felt by every cell and damages every cell.

One of the most basic ways to be aware is by grounding yourself in the body. There is no mystery to this. Simply tune in to the feelings in your body whenever you've been distracted. Let's say you're driving a car and somebody cuts you off. Your normal reaction is to be agitated or angry;

when you feel this way, you lose the calm, relaxed focus that connects you to the field. So try this: instead of being disrupted by this disruption, just go within and feel the sensations of your body. Take a deep breath, since that is an easy way to come back to body awareness.

Keep your attention on these distracting sensations until they disappear. What you've done is break the chain of stimulus-response by creating a gap, an interval of nonreaction. This stops the reaction from fueling itself. It reminds the body of its natural state of harmonious, coordinated self-regulation. And that grounds you. Harmonious self-regulation is the body's ground state. Stress pulls you into another state, of heightened biological responses that trigger a flow of hormones, increase heart rate, stimulate hypervigilance of the senses, and many other linked reactions. But these are all temporary; they are emergency measures only. If you allow the stress reaction to become a habit, however, disharmony enters the field. The normal state of relaxed awareness tries to coexist with the agitated state of the stress response, but the two don't mix; they aren't meant to exist at the same time.

Anytime you're feeling distracted, overwhelmed, stressed, or overshadowed, there's a tendency to escape. Denial is a form of escape. Distracting yourself through overwork is an escape. Altering your mind with drugs and alcohol is an escape. What they all have in common is absence of awareness. You numb or distract yourself under the false belief that being too aware will only increase your pain. In reality the opposite is true. Awareness heals, because awareness is truly whole, and healing is fundamentally a return to wholeness.

Science is just beginning to understand the phenomenon of healing. Over millions of years our bodies evolved to regulate thousands of microscopic processes simultaneously. Disease occurs when the body forgets how to self-regulate itself. Healing occurs when the body remembers how to self-regulate itself.

You can be exposed to pneumococcus bacteria, for example, but exposure alone isn't enough to create infection. You don't contract pneumonia if your body knows how to make the appropriate antibody, and that ability ultimately comes down to awareness. Your immune system recognizes an invader, identifies it, and calls for the appropriate intervention. These are all conscious acts. Healing therefore cannot be understood unless the mind is as fully conscious as the body. In medicine we have isolated the nervous system, the endocrine system, the cardiovascular system, but we ignore the healing system. It's invisible, it includes every part of the body, it responds to the ghostly wisp of thought and feeling. Yet nothing is more intelligent, creative, and powerful than the healing system, the one thing we keep ignoring.

Healing should be as constant as breathing, not an isolated process for fending off illness. Healing should mean constant communication with the field. We've covered the most important step: becoming aware of the sensations in your body. The other thing you can do is begin to become aware of the field that invisibly unifies everything. How is that done? Ordinarily you focus on things, people, and events—all kinds of outward stimuli. Instead, *try looking at the spaces between things*. If you're looking at another person, shift your attention to the space between the two of you. The field exists where we think there is nothing—in the space between thoughts, the space between objects, the space between breaths, the space between movements. It's all the same space, but what we call nothing is lack of awareness. If you are aware, space is full, rich, dynamic. It's the field of pure potential, the unknown region from which the next moment and everything in it will emerge.

Space is always still. So when you bring your attention to space, you still the mind. At the same time your body can begin to release the stored-up frustration, tension, and residues of past stress. In this state of deep relaxation, healing becomes most active. Your body needs to release the energy that is stuck to outworn emotions, memories, and traumas. Ideally, you wouldn't identify with these negative influences; you wouldn't hold on to them and add more energy to them. But we all do. We keep the body from relaxing by constantly putting excessive demands, both conscious and unconscious, upon it.

If you don't think your body is operating under the burden of such demands, you can prove this quite easily. Just relax, sit quietly, and tell your body that it can do anything it wants. One of the following is likely to happen: deep sighs, drowsiness, a rush of memory, unexpected physical sensations (usually discomfort or tightness), spontaneous emotion, perhaps tears, and a sense of relief. These are all signals from your body that it needs space to heal and refresh itself.

If your body is actually in a natural state that is self-healing without resistance, the experiment will produce the opposite effect. If you sit still and tell your body to do whatever it wants, one or more of the following will result: a sense of deep stillness and peace; faint effervescence; lightness; bubbling joy, however faint; and a sense of wonder at the unknown that is peering through the mask of material existence.

In other words, when your body is in a natural state, you are experiencing happiness. When you're happy at this effortless level, you regain the memory of who you really are. Your consciousness is fulfilled, because in every cell there is a state of knowingness, joy, and the certainty of immortality. In India we call this *Sat Chit Ananda*, or eternal bliss consciousness. In this state of being, your body heals itself simply by knowing itself. What does it know? That the greatest attributes of the divine—omniscience, omnipotence, and omnipresence—are actually the most basic stuff of life.

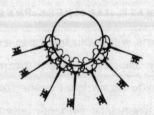

To Activate the *First Key*
in Everyday Life, I Promise Myself
to Do the Following:

1. I will make choices to maximize the energy in my body. My body is my connection to the universe's infinite supply of energy. If I am feeling lack of energy in any way, it means that I am resisting the flow of this infinite supply. I will ask my body what it needs and will follow its advice. The ideal state is to experience such lightness that I do not feel bounded by my body. It and the universe are one.

2. Before I act on any emotion, I will consult my heart. My heart is a reliable guide when I put my trust in it. It helps me experience empathy, compassion, and love. The heart is the seat of emotional intelligence. Emotional intelligence allows me to get in touch with my deepest self. It nurtures all relationships by reminding me to see myself in the other.

3. Lightness of being in my body will be my indicator of happiness. If I feel heavy or dull in my body, I will pay special attention, because these feelings are signs that I am suffering from inertia and the force of habit rather than experiencing the potential in every moment for freshness and new life. The best way to replenish my body is to give it what it needs most, whether it's sleep, rest, life-giving nourishment, the joy of movement, or communion with Nature.

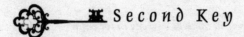 **Second Key**

FIND TRUE SELF-ESTEEM

True self-esteem is not the same thing as improving your self-image. Self-image results from what other people think of you. The true self lies beyond images. It can be found at a level of existence that is independent of the good and bad opinions of others. It is fearless. It has infinite worth. When you shift your identity from your self-image to your true self, you will find happiness that no one can take away from you.

You yourself, as much as anybody in the entire universe, deserve your love and affection.

—Buddha

Do not wish to be anything but what you are, and try to be that perfectly.

—St. Francis de Sales

Happiness is natural to life because it is part of the self. When you know yourself, you access happiness at its source. But most people confuse themselves with their self-image. Our self-image is created when we identify with external things. These can be people, events, and situations as well as physical objects. People seek money, for instance, in the belief that the more they have, the happier they'll be. Even though we've all heard that money can't buy happiness, the pursuit of money hasn't ended, because we identify so strongly with how much money we earn, how good our job is, and what kinds of things we own. Money, status, possessions, and the opinions of others have a powerful influence on who we think we are.

One side of the coin is that we crave approval because it bolsters our self-image. The other side is that we fear disapproval because it diminishes our self-image. All of this is known as object-referral, which means that you identify with objects outside yourself. The opposite of object-referral is self-referral, which means you identify with your true being, entirely an inner experience. True being has five qualities, none of which is created by external things, events, or other people.

1. Your true being is connected to all that exists.
2. It has no limitations.
3. It has infinite creativity.
4. It is fearless, and willing to step into the unknown.
5. Intention from the level of being is powerful and can orchestrate synchronicity (a perfect meshing of outside circumstances to bring about your intention).

Shifting your sense of identity to your true being frees you to create a life of abundance, joy, and fulfillment. Being tied to external things leaves you stranded on a superficial level of existence. You don't have to live there. At a deeper level of existence you can manifest your deepest desires. Once you allow it to, your true being can create the situations, circumstances, and relationships in your life.

When you aren't manifesting your deepest desires, the root cause is that you have mistaken who you really are. Object-referral pulls us out of true identity into false identity. In India this state is known as *avidyā*, or absence of true knowledge. An ancient saying compares avidyā to a millionaire walking the streets like a beggar because he's forgotten he has untold wealth in the bank.

When you don't remember who you really are, you have no choice but to fall back upon your ego. Object-referral creates an ego identity from all the events and circumstances of your past, starting the day you were born. If you look closely, the ego is actually quite insecure. It is addicted to approval, control, security, and power. There's nothing wrong with any of these things. The problem is becoming addicted to them to the point that without approval, control, security, and power, you feel lost and afraid. As with any addiction, at first there's a sense of pleasure when the ego is in charge: "I'm in control; others give in to what I want." "I'm secure because no one challenges me." "I'm powerful because others feel inferior in my presence." The ego tries to construct all these situations, and it can achieve them, at least partially. Yet very soon the pleasure goes away, eroded by gnawing doubt and fear. Those we control and have power over might turn the tables, and then look what happens.

If you want to know how strongly you identify with your ego as opposed to your true being, there's no mystery about it. The ego has the opposite qualities from the five we described before.

1. The ego feels isolated and alone. Therefore it needs outside validation in order to belong and have worth.

2. The ego feels limited and bounded. Without power and control over others, it fears that its helplessness will be exposed.

3. The ego prefers routine and habit over creativity. It finds security in making today the same as the day before.

4. The ego fears the unknown more than anything else. This is because it sees the unknown as a place of darkness and emptiness.

5. The ego struggles to get what it wants. It assumes that without struggle, its needs would never be fulfilled; this reflects a deep sense of inner lack.

As you can see, the central theme of the ego is insecurity. Living your life from the ego puts you at the mercy of every stranger on the street. A moment of flattery creates happiness; a sarcastic comment, and you are wounded. So how do we shift to our true being? Many people try to make such a shift by fighting against the ego, but this is a trap. This is the ultimate melodrama of the ego, to constantly struggle and never reach real fulfillment, peace, and happiness. In any case, the ego will resist the shift you want to make, because it senses its own destruction in your search to find your true being.

This fear is totally unfounded. True being achieves everything the ego wants—peace, fulfillment, joy, a sense of complete security—because all of those qualities reside in being. You don't have to struggle to find them. So the real problem is that the path your ego has set you on was the wrong path to begin with. The ego becomes depressed when it can't get what it wants; it feels like a failure. What it fails to realize is that you don't fail when what you wanted was unattainable to begin with.

The ego was never on the right path. Object-referral will never lead to security and safety, fulfillment and satisfaction. So the real question is how to coax the ego out of its misguided ways while at the same time ending this lifelong habit of identifying with external objects.

First, notice what you are doing. Remember, awareness is the key to change. Almost everyone goes around trying to earn the approval of others, repeating a pattern that goes back to infancy, when we felt we had to earn our parents' love. Without it, we would feel totally lost; we even thought we'd die—and we might have. But now we are adults. Notice how easily you are still wounded by small slights, how deeply unhappy you still feel when someone you love doesn't pay enough attention to you or seems to move away. Become aware of these habitual feelings. The memory of being wounded in the past makes you place undue importance on what a stranger thinks of you. A child's emotional neediness makes it hard to accept that someone you love may simply need some space now and then.

Once you open the door to awareness, don't fight against the fear and insecurity you have released. Awareness has healing power if you simply look and allow. A painful slight comes your way; you feel wounded. Be with that feeling and it will dissipate. Your ego wants you to remember the past out of a mistaken belief that you must keep defending yourself over and over. Remembering what hurt us before, we direct our energies toward making certain that an old hurt will not repeat itself. But trying to impose the past on the present will never wipe out the threat of being hurt.

To correct this mistake, just ask yourself, "Do I recognize this feeling of being wounded? Is it old or new?" If you are being honest, you will immediately see that it's a very old feeling. The past is reaching out to grab you. Now ask the next question: "How much good has it ever done me to remember my old hurts?" Again, if you are honest, you will see that it has done you no good whatever. If recalling old hurts prevented you from being hurt here and now, you wouldn't feel so bad. You wouldn't be so vulnerable to external disapproval. If your ego was on the right path, it wouldn't have this toxic storehouse of old pain.

Using simple awareness you can defuse old hurts by no longer clinging to the belief that they are doing you some good. The ego has many subtle ways of persuading you that you must repeat today all the tactics that didn't work yesterday. Instead of playing its game, just witness what is going on. You will find it challenging to see through the whole game, because it has its positive side. Your past also contains moments of joy, success, love, and fulfillment. Dredging up those positive experiences, the ego whispers, "See? You're on the right track. I will bring you more of the same. Trust me."

By bringing up insecurity from the past but mixing it with memories of fulfillment, the ego convinces you of an illusion: that one day your self-image will be ideal. You will look in the mirror and see only the good things that created your self-image and none of the bad. Ironically, by pursuing an ideal, you wind up losing your true self, which is ideal to begin with.

Instead of trying to live up to your ideal self-image, surrender to the simplicity and innocence of being. Once you know who you really are, being is enough. There is no need for struggle. Your true self is the self of the universe. What more can you want? When you have creativity, feel fearless, can step into the unknown, and have the power of intention, everything has been given to you.

Awareness requires practice and patience. It takes time for the fruit to ripen before it falls. But as the process deepens, you will notice more ease, lightheartedness, joy, and synchronicity in your life. These are signs that you are connected to your true being.

Remember, the ego has been shaping your sense of self for many years. It has become second nature. Even after people accept the vision of a true self, they go around fighting against their bad habits, adopting regimens and disciplines that are supposed to bring self-actualization. But consider what it means to be self-actualized. A self-actualized person is somebody who needs no approval and is free of both criticism and flattery, someone who feels neither superior to anyone nor inferior to anyone, someone who experiences what it's like to act fearlessly because they are detached from the influence of situations, circumstances, events, and relationships. We can't build those qualities from the materials the ego supplies. Everything your true self stands for is independent of the image the ego has so carefully assembled to feel good about itself.

It helps to keep in mind what is real and what is illusory:

Abundance is real. Lack is an illusion.
Being good is real. Trying to be good is an illusion.
Surrender is real. Holding on is an illusion.
This moment is real. The past is an illusion.
You are real. Who you think you are is an illusion.

Self-referral allows you to see—and to accept—reality. By turning outside yourself, you are only reinforcing unreality. And unreality, unfortunately, is what our culture is selling. Whenever you find yourself trying to impress somebody else, stop for a moment. Consider what's going on. Ask yourself, "Why does this person care if I am better or worse than he is? Because we are both buying into the same external references. He needs me as much as I need him." Notice how much effort you are spending to impress people who will then turn around and try to impress someone else. The cycle never ends, because it's based on mutual insecurity.

When you make the shift to self-referral, however, this self-defeating behavior ends. You alone are the judge of your worth, and your goal is to discover infinite worth in yourself, no matter what anyone else thinks. There is great freedom in this realization. I remember reading about a great Russian pianist whose talent awed everyone, even his rivals. He had learned almost every piece of classical music and had total recall. His technique was superhuman. Fiendishly difficult passages were child's play to him. Yet when he came to visit friends, he made no demands for respect and admiration. He never drew attention to himself. When it was time to go to bed, he was satisfied to curl up in a blanket underneath the piano in the living room.

You can imagine how his friends regarded him. They had even more awe and respect for the great man than if he had demanded it, or thought he deserved it. In innocence and simplicity there is natural greatness. You can't create this quality. Your being radiates it, and only by discovering your being can you radiate the beauty and truth that are natural to life.

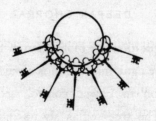

To Activate the *Second Key* in Everyday Life, I Promise Myself to Do the Following:

1. I will observe myself in difficult situations without judgment. I will simply witness myself until I no longer feel pressured and distressed. Because the ego is a very constricted version of my true self, it creates a sensation of tightness and contraction in the body. This is usually felt in the chest, heart, stomach, solar plexus, shoulders, neck, or back. Whenever my ego self is trying to dominate a situation, I will feel discomfort in one of these places. At such a moment, it is enough to be aware that my ego is creating the sensation. By observing what the ego is doing, I can separate from a false sense of self.

2. I will question my motivation in the choices I make. The ego's motivation is always rooted in its addiction to power, control, security, and approval. The true self is always motivated by love. Today I will begin to shift to my true self by being aware of my motivations and noticing how much is love and how much is ego.

3. I will recapitulate my day when I go to bed at night, observing every event of the day as a neutral observer. I will do this for five minutes, letting the whole day unspool like a movie in my mind. As I watch I will ask to become aware of where I was acting out of ego and where I was acting from my true self.

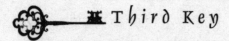 *Third* Key

DETOXIFY
YOUR LIFE

Your natural state is one of joy, peace, and
spontaneous fulfillment. When you are not
experiencing this state, some contamination is
present in body or mind. Contamination can
be the result of toxic emotions, habits, and
relationships, as well as toxic substances. All of
these are rooted first in the mind as the result
of conditioning. Therefore, the solution to toxicity
in your life lies at the level where the mind has
lost its natural state. Such conditioning begins
very early in life. The first symptoms are toxic
emotions like anger, anxiety, guilt, and shame.
As one grows, this is followed by poor self-esteem,
toxic relationships, and lifestyle imbalances.
In order to detoxify your life, you need to learn
how to reverse this entire range of conditioning.

*Who shall ascend to the hill of the Lord? Or who
shall stand in his holy place? He who has clean
hands and a pure heart.*

—Psalm 24

Τhe roots of unhappiness are often invisible. This is especially true of the conditioning that creates toxicity in a person's life. The most powerful conditioning exists at a subtle level of the mind. It begins in the first year of a child's life, as the infant brain learns how to think, feel, and behave from influences in the home. Conditioning becomes a dominant feature in all of us by the time we're toddlers.

This is when we set lifelong patterns into our brains. Even today you are replaying scenarios you learned when you were two or three. Consider a small child out with his mother. He sees a giant lollipop and wants one. What does he do? The most common pattern is the following: First he is nice, asking in a cajoling voice if Mommy will buy him a lollipop. If this tactic doesn't work, he tries the opposite, acting nasty. He whines and cries and makes a scene. If this doesn't work, the next step is to become stubborn and indifferent. He refuses to pay attention to his mother, who wants him to stop being unhappy and difficult. This is a subtler approach than nice or nasty. If stubbornness fails, the last scenario is to play the victim—poor me, no one loves me enough to buy me a lollipop. When the mother finally gives in, her child becomes conditioned, thinking he's discovered something that "works."

Simple as this emotional cycle might sound, millions of adults continue to act it out, using the same belief that their tactics "work" to get them what they want. The problem with this conditioning is that by manipulating others, you never really get what you want, which is greater love, peace, and joy. Because conditioning trains the brain into a false sense of happiness, you are actually manipulating yourself. You become the kind of person who doesn't know how to be anything other than nice, nasty, stubborn, or a victim.

Conditioning is the subtlest form of toxicity. You cannot reach true happiness without escaping your mental conditioning. In our society there's a wave of interest in leading a life that's more natural, free of toxic substances. Purification of every type can be beneficial. But the secret to detoxifying your body lies more in the mind than anywhere else. There are seven steps to ridding yourself of a toxin at the subtle level:

Step 1. *Take responsibility for your present response.*

Step 2. *Witness what you are feeling.*

Step 3. *Label your feeling.*

Step 4. *Express what you feel.*

Step 5. *Share what you feel.*

Step 6. *Release the toxic feeling through ritual.*

Step 7. *Celebrate the release and move on.*

These seven steps apply whether you are trying to change a toxic emotion, habit, craving, or relationship, because your past conditioning lies at the heart of all of them.

Take responsibility. First, give up blame and guilt.
Escaping your unhappiness today means finding a creative way to alter your own conditioned response, which is rooted in yesterday. When you don't take responsibility, you are putting your fate into someone else's hands. If you blame someone else, you are waiting for that person to change so that you can feel better. How long does that take? You could be waiting for the rest of your life. It's difficult enough to change yourself. Release the need to change anyone else.

Witness your feeling. Conditioning trains you to
feel the same way over and over every time you meet the same situation. This is frustrating because as soon as the old response rises, you become tangled in it. What you need is a clear place, the place of witnessing. Witnessing means that

you are present with your emotion but not being used by it. The best way to witness is to locate where the feeling is in your body. Toxic emotions are usually located in one of the subtle centers known in Sanskrit as the chakras. Anger is felt in the gut, nervousness in the stomach, fear in the heart, frustration in the throat, sexual tension in the genital area. There's no need to get complicated here, however. When asked what kind of toxic feeling they have, most people come up with fear and anger. When you have those feelings, don't get involved in "what" they are saying. Instead, feel "where" in our body they are saying it. Locating a feeling in your body bypasses the inner mental chatter that keeps such feelings alive.

Label your feeling. Whatever sensation you find in your body, give it a name. Use very simple words: *fear, anger, hostility, frustration, shame, guilt, jealousy*. Don't use judgmental words like *betrayed, disappointed,* and *hurt*—any word that implies blaming someone else. Naming your feeling is a way of recognizing what you are dealing with. Because you are being simple—and truthful—you aren't falling for the long, complicated story that we are all tempted to rehash when we get upset. Every story is about one thing, the past. Your sensations and emotions are in the present.

Express the feeling. Any emotion becomes more toxic when you bottle it up. Expressing it leads to release, which is purifying to body and mind. This step isn't about expressing how much you hate or blame someone else, but since you naturally want to tell your side, first express your feeling from your point of view by writing it down. Then express it from the other person's point of view, which is more difficult. Then write down your position from a third-party perspective, as if you were covering it for the *New York Times*. When you go through all three perspectives, the conflict, anger, or fear you are feeling begins to lose its energy. You have expanded your awareness. Expansion allows trapped energy to flow; contraction keeps the energy bottled up to fester. This is a useful rule, because everyone's first reaction is to contract into a single point of view, their own.

Share your feeling. Now expand beyond your private perspective, allowing others to participate. Share your feeling with someone you trust. Share the whole process you have been going through, including all three points of view. Don't just gripe or make the case for your own point of view. Your aim is to get a true reflection, which the right listener can provide.

Let go through ritual. Devise your own ceremony that symbolically purifies your life of this particular toxin. You are invoking the age-old power of symbols, part of every culture. Having gone through this process, you will find that you no longer need to hold on. You would rather be the person who is free of this toxic feeling. Come up with a ritual that you will remember and that is significant for you personally—throwing a note in the river, giving your burden to the Virgin Mary, tossing your grievance into the sea wrapped around a rock—whatever ritual allows you to say, "From this moment on I'm free." You can do this privately, but many people want witnesses to validate their release and help them to remember its significance.

Celebrate and move on. Now it's time to honor your release through shared joy and gratitude. You will be celebrating an ending and a beginning. The occasion doesn't have to be boisterous or showy. You are giving a gift to yourself. This is symbolic in its importance, because in celebration you validate that you deserve to be free and happy. Then move on.

Not everyone is comfortable with all seven steps. Try them out anyway, because conditioning has a habit of saying, "You don't need to change. You're okay the way you are." But if you are feeling discouraged, depressed, and anxious, that voice is lying. However familiar it sounds, it's the voice of defeat; it is working against your happiness.

These seven steps allow you to establish new patterns for coping in a new way. Don't rush through them or be tempted to skip ahead. Let each step have its own integrity. That is the only way to escape the past, which is by filling in the present with new behavior. The time may come when you don't have to go through all seven steps because you've become skilled at recognizing your feelings, witnessing them, and then moving the toxic energy that glues them in place. Eventually you may find that you can automatically see your situation from several points of view. For now, though, be dedicated to every step of inner purification.

Once you start to feel emotionally free because you are no longer holding on, you have opened the space to detoxify your life in general. You will find that you want simplicity in your life, because happiness is simple. Before, it was easy to become entangled in superfluous things at every level—too many activities, possessions, buried feelings, and decisions that never get made. When you're ready, however, everything superfluous can be released. Here's a basic checklist.

1. Declutter your surroundings.
2. If you buy something, give something away.
3. Spend money to help the environment, returning a fraction of Nature's gifts to you.
4. Do something that's not for profit.
5. Be generous.
6. Be lavish in your giving, particularly with intangibles.
7. Nourish your body instead of defiling it.

Life is either complicated and getting more complicated, or it's simple and getting simpler. The main thing is to move from the first state to the second. Emotional conditioning is where it begins, always. Therefore, every time you escape your old conditioning, even in tiny ways that may not seem that significant, you are forming more efficient neural networks in your brain. In plain language, you are becoming clearheaded. Instead of feeling undecided between *A* or *B,* you are teaching your brain to feel the world directly. This new way of feeling has limitless possibilities. That's the difference between being conditioned and being unconditioned—in the latter state you give yourself so much more of life's infinite potential. In the end, there is only one toxin. It's whatever robs you of your true self. Your true self breathes in complete freedom of choice. Every day it grows toward untold possibilities. When you finally become free of all conditioning, you will be true and purified at the same time.

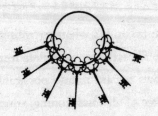

To Activate the *Third* Key
in Everyday Life, I Promise Myself
to Do the Following:

1. I will pay attention to the seven-step process whenever a toxic emotion comes up. This begins by taking responsibility for my own responses and not blaming others. Any response that makes me unhappy is mine to change. I will find the power to change by escaping my old conditioning, which keeps me unhappy. This is the most potent way to detoxify.

2. Before I put anything in my body, I will ask if it is nourishing me or not. Nourishment can come in the form of pure food but also pure emotions and all healing influences. I will not force any habit to change. If I am adding anything toxic to my life—whether in the form of substances, emotions, or relationships—I will not fight against my impulses. Instead, I will discover change at the root cause, which is emotional conditioning.

3. I will take a step to simplify my life. Whenever I see that anything has become too complicated, I see that it is leading only to more complications. My aim is to be free of the superfluous things that weigh me down. First comes simplicity of spirit, which has nothing to do with externals and everything to do with the happiness that accompanies my true self.

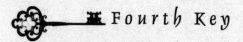 Fourth Key

GIVE UP
BEING RIGHT

An enormous amount of energy becomes
available once you give up the need to be right.
Being right implies that someone else must
be wrong. All relationships are damaged by
a confrontation between right and wrong.
The result is great suffering and conflict in the
world. To give up the need to be right doesn't
mean that you don't have a point of view. But
you can give up your need to defend your point
of view. In a state of defenselessness, we find
invincibility, because there is no longer anything
to attack. We are all a single consciousness
with unique ways of experiencing the world.
Wholeness is a state of profound peace
and happiness.

If you never assume importance, you never lose it.
                                    —Tao Te Ching

He who accepts Nature's flow is all-cherishing.
                                    —Tao Te Ching

Most people are trapped trying to impose their viewpoint on the world. They carry around beliefs about what is right and wrong, and they hold on to these beliefs for years. "I am right" brings comfort, but not true happiness. The people you feel wronged by will never apologize and make your wounds and grievances go away. The people you judge against will remain isolated from you. No one has ever been made happy by proving that they are right. The only result is conflict and confrontation, because the need to be right always makes someone else wrong.

There is no such thing as one and only one correct perspective. Right is whatever conforms to your perception. You see the world as you are. Others see the world as they are, too. This insight is tremendously liberating because, first of all, it makes you unique. Ultimately it makes you a cocreator with God. For as your consciousness expands, so does reality. Tremendous hidden potential is revealed.

The opposite happens if you insist upon being right. Because others will disagree, your need to be right will generate antagonism and rejection. As we are all too sadly aware, if the need to be right is rigid and fierce enough, wars ensue, often in the name of God. If the world is a mirror of who you are, it is always reflecting a point of view. Objectivity is an illusion of the ego, created to bolster its insistence that what it sees is right. It's tragic that people sacrifice the real goal of life, which is increasing joy and happiness, for the cold comfort of judging others and feeling superior to them. If you see the world with judgment instead of love, that's the world you will inhabit.

Conflicts arise as a result of not understanding that there are as many points of view as there are people. Our unique points of view are a gift. We live in a universe reflecting who we are, which we should cherish and celebrate. Instead, we rush to defend our tiny piece of it. Consider how relationships develop. We get along well with someone else who agrees with our point of view. We feel an intimate connection; we feel validated in their presence. Then the spell is broken: it turns out that the other person has many opinions and beliefs with which we don't agree at all. At this point, the war between right and wrong starts, and the road to unhappiness unspools before us.

The very fact that you are in an intimate relationship makes it even more painful to find areas of disagreement. At the subtle emotional level you feel abandoned. The beautiful sense of merging with someone you love is shattered. At this point love is compromised, as both people experience the return of the ego, which says, "I am right. My way of doing things is the only way. If you really loved me, you'd give in." But in reality love hasn't failed. It was just blocked by the need to be right, to cling to your own viewpoint instead of surrendering to what love would do. To the ego, however, surrender is defeat and disgrace.

If you are mindful of this fact, then every time the urge to be right surfaces in your awareness, look at your circumstances in context. Is it possible that someone else's viewpoint is as valid as yours? Since the equality of viewpoints is a given, now it becomes possible to let go of the win-lose scenario. Ask yourself, "What do I really want out of the situation, to be right or to be happy?" Can you see that the two are not the same? When you give in to your need to be right, you are turning your back on love, communion, and ultimately unity. Unity is the realization that at the deepest level everyone shares the same consciousness, which is the source of all love and joy.

The more you accept this, the less need you will have to be judgmental. As your experience of not needing to be right deepens, the mind becomes quieter. You start to feel more empathy, and your perception widens. A knowingness arises that encloses both you and the person who disagrees with you. As you relax and become less defensive, you lose your obsession with definitions, labels, descriptions, evaluations, analysis, and judgment. These are all part of the ego's battery of defenses. They work tremendously well in starting arguments and wars; they work miserably in bringing about peace.

When the need to be right fades, we no longer have so many grievances and resentments, which are the fallout of making someone else wrong. It takes a perception of wrong to create victims. But aren't there real victims in the world, people who have received terrible injustice and ill treatment? The injustice is very real and undeniable. But the label of "victim" is something else—it's a psychological wound. A person scarred by it cannot help but construct a story that every new experience reinforces: "I am hurt by life, my situation is weak and wounded. I resent those who have power over me. My grievance has become who I am." In the end, to be a victim is actually a form of self-judgment. In the name of having been wounded, you wound yourself every day by assuming the victim's role.

Going beyond resentment detaches you from anger and hostility. Anger closes the door to the realm of spirit. As much as you feel justified in harboring your grievances, at a deeper level you have tied yourself to the one who injured you. That connection becomes so important that it obscures the connection to spirit, your higher self, and your soul. People frequently use spirituality to justify their moral outrage at the world's inhumanity, which falls so horribly short of the ideal. While it is easy to have empathy for this perspective, it's also important to recognize that even moral outrage is rage. Since consciousness is a field that embraces everyone, the result is that even more anger, resentment, and hostility are being added to the field.

Outrage tends to become an excuse for inaction. The people who actually combat the world's injustice are not consumed by anger. They are clearheaded, self-possessed, and certain as to where their values lie. They can distinguish between what is past and gone, about which nothing can be done, and what is present and therefore correctable. Einstein famously said, "No problem can be solved at the level of consciousness in which it was conceived." This is worth remembering whenever you are tempted to rationalize your anger as righteous. Righteousness never solved anything. It just fuels more anger; it provokes deeper antagonism. Above all, it defies Einstein's rule: The level of the solution is always different from the level of the problem.

To get beyond the level of the problem, you must see

yourself clearly. Many people don't even know when they are defending their need to be right. The signs are not always anger and resentment. But righteous behavior always has one common denominator: the refusal to surrender. Only surrender brings freedom from judgment. When you are dominated by your ego, surrender feels like total defeat. The ego thrives under the following conditions:

You get what you want.

Others agree to follow your agenda.

There is a sense of self-control.

Right and wrong are clearly demarcated.

Nobody crosses the line between right and wrong.

You name the conditions of loving someone else and
*   being loved in return.*

Anyone who agrees with you is showing that he/she
*   loves you.*

Someone who obeys you feels safe. Someone you must
*   obey feels unsafe.*

Ironically, these conditions for making your ego happy turn out to make who you really are very unhappy. There is no joy in being in charge, no love in controlling others, no expansion in defending the line between right and wrong.

So seductive is the ego's story, however, that countless people pursue happiness in the ways described. And they may even achieve perfect self-discipline and power over others, but in so doing they will sacrifice their true selves.

To find your true self, you must surrender to it, and the best way to do that is to surrender to another person. This doesn't mean that one ego gives in to another ego. That would indeed spell defeat. Instead, you share with the other person the truth about yourself.

You want love without limitations.
You want to feel safe.
You want to express yourself creatively.
You want to expand in joy.
You want to be free.
You highest wish is for unity in a state of perfect peace.

When you can share these deep desires with another, what happens? The same thing that has always been happening. The world will reflect your level of consciousness. In this case, the reflection comes from one other person— the one who shares your truth. When you say to your beloved, "You are my world," you are being quite literal.

But this is only the first stage of surrender. It isn't

possible for two people to want the same thing every minute of the day. Both want different things; both have different points of view. To carry surrender beyond being merely an ideal, it must be made practical. Many people want to have a spiritual relationship, only to founder on the many obstacles that arise in everyday life—issues over money, career, family, and ambitions, for instance. There is no need to suppress these issues, or to settle for compromises that don't fully satisfy either party. If you cannot fulfill yourself, you can't possibly fulfill another.

The secret isn't to surrender to another person, or even to each other. You surrender to the path. It is a path you share. Your commitment is not to what you want or to what your partner wants. Individual desire is secondary. You commit to wherever the path is taking you. In this way you give up your ego-centered perspective. Your focus shifts to the space between you and the one you love. This is the gap between ego and spirit. Whenever you are tempted to obey your ego, you go to this shared space and ask the following:

Which choice is more loving?
What will bring peace between us?
How awake am I?

What kind of energy am I creating?
Am I acting out of trust or distrust?
Do I feel what my partner is feeling?
Can I give without expecting anything in return?

These questions don't have automatic answers. They serve instead to wake you up spiritually. They attune you to a process that is more than "me" and "you." The space you share with someone else allows you to look beyond ego. The advantage of doing this isn't obvious at first. Your old conditioning will say, "What's wrong with getting what I want? Why should I consider someone else before me? I have a right to expect good things for myself."

What your ego cannot see is something precious that is hidden in every spiritual relationship: mystery. This mystery is born of love; it calls to you from a place of peace and joy that the ego can never reach with all its struggles, demands, and needs. Simply by entering the space between you and someone you love, you open yourself to the mystery. When two people fall in love, the existence of the mystery is obvious; it all but blinds them. They feel merged and perfected in their state of rapture. Nothing can ever go wrong. The whole world exists in the other person. But when romance fades, this certainty fades with it. So it takes commitment to keep alive those first glimpses of a fulfillment that lies beyond yourself, yet is nothing but yourself.

When you commit to the path, you also surrender to it. Every day you ask, "What can love do? Show me. I am ready." The answers will surprise you. Love can solve problems, heal wounds, settle disputes, and bring unexpected answers. Here we aren't talking about personal love, the feeling contained inside a single person. This is a love beyond the personal that watches and knows everything. When you give yourself to it, everyday differences mean very little: money, ambition, career, family concerns all fall into place. An invisible power reconciles opposites; it creates harmony of its own accord.

To experience such a state, you cannot work for it or try to control it. You allow yourself to be in a state of openness. You witness what is going on; you hang loose; you obey when the right impulse takes hold. This is how life is lived spontaneously. Whatever happens next is the right thing. Whatever you need at the deepest level is automatically given. It is possible to exist in such a state, although few people do. In fact, it is the most natural way to live. But if you judge your life, if you hold on to being right, if you insist on setting boundaries, then the mystery cannot reach you. Living in harmony with the mystery takes time. Surrender, like everything else, is a process, not a leap. Despite ups and downs, the path always goes forward, and every step is a step of love. Ultimately that is the reason for relationships, to be able to look into someone else's eyes and share the knowledge that the power of love has blessed you both.

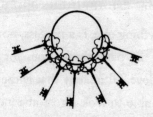

To Activate the Fourth Key
in Everyday Life, I Promise Myself
to Do the Following:

1. I will catch myself wanting to be right. When this happens, I will observe the impulse and let it go. In witnessing this behavior, I begin my transformation. Every reminder will reinforce my goal in life, which is to be happy, not to be right.

2. I will refrain from qualifying things as right and wrong, good and bad. I will find freedom in a wider perspective that leads to creative solutions rather than judgments and accusations. My happiness lies in the calm stillness that lies beyond all labels.

3. When I am tempted to see myself as a victim, I will remember that I am the creator of the circumstances I see. I will ask myself, "What am I doing in a state of consciousness where I am creating this?" Just by asking this question, I will shift from being a victim to being a creator.

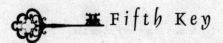 Fifth Key

FOCUS ON THE PRESENT

If you focus on the present, your life will
be constantly renewed. The present moment
is the only time that is eternal. It never dies,
nor can it be forgotten. Therefore, happiness
in the present can never be taken away from
you. It will free you from the snare of time,
which brings about suffering through thought,
evaluation, and analysis. Being fully in
the present, you experience the timeless.
In the timeless you find your true self.

There will never be any more perfection than
there is now.

—*from "Song of Myself," Walt Whitman*

Although we have all heard that we should live in the present and not in the past, there is a deeper spiritual lesson to be found in those words. Before a thought arises in your mind, you are in a timeless state. After a thought has served its purpose, whether it brings up a desire or the memory of a past event, you return to that state of timelessness. There, you don't need a reason to be happy. You just are.

Happiness based on reasons is actually another form of misery. Whatever the reason for your happiness—a good relationship, a pleasurable situation, or material possessions—it can be taken away from you at any moment. Therefore, your happiness is fragile and dependent on externals. Happiness without reasons is real happiness. It is frequently referred to as bliss. This is a happiness that can never be taken away.

You don't need to seek bliss, nor do you need to feel nostalgic once you've experienced it. Bliss is available in the now. So what is the now? We can call it present-moment awareness, which is a good phrase, because it reminds us that bliss cannot be found by remembering the past or anticipating the future. The present has no time span. The instant you try to measure the present moment, it disappears. So the now is ever renewing. It is timeless because time cannot stop it. The now can never grow old or die.

Time is a mysterious phenomenon, but we know that it is subjective, and we use it to measure experience. Consider the following sentences:

I was having a good time and the hours flew by.
I was bored and time dragged.
I was on a tight deadline and time was running out.
*The beauty of the mountains was so breathtaking that
time stood still.*

Each of these experiences of time is personal. The whole problem of time is that we always make it personal. Whether you regret something in your past or worry about something in the future, you are creating changes in your body. In other words, you are spending much of your life metabolizing time. Every experience in your life has been metabolized in your physical body and influences your biological clock. In fact, biological aging, with all its consequences of infirmity, suffering, and unhappiness, is nothing other than the metabolism of time. Even the momentary recall of a past trauma makes you suffer all over again. Good experiences are also the metabolism of time, but they don't put wear and tear on the body.

The wisdom traditions of the world put enormous attention on solving the problem of time because bliss, the kind of happiness that needs no reasons, can only happen in the present moment. If your life is trapped in the passage of time, your body will also be trapped. But if you can escape the clutches of time, your body will be transformed by the experience of bliss.

Here is the solution that the wisdom traditions arrived at.

Time, they said, is the movement of consciousness, or put simply, the movement of thought. The real you, which lies beyond thought, can only be found in the now. Your true self, existing in the eternal now, is neither an observer nor an object of observation. As soon as a thought arises in your mind, however, an observer appears, along with the object of observation. Thus we find that each person exists in two realities. First, the silent state of being that is not captured by time; this is the home of bliss. Second, the relative world full of experience; the mind lives in this world by constantly acting as the observer focused on an object of observation.

When you put your focus on the present, you are aligning yourself with the first reality and its potential for happiness that can never be taken away. But if you focus on the second reality, with its constant change of scenery, your mind will be captivated by time. Time will then bring about all the negative effects we have already mentioned.

When you focus on the present moment, you don't give up the relative world. You will still participate in everyday life, but with a difference. You will no longer identify with change. The ups and downs of fortune will not shake you from your true self. Ordinarily, we are so caught up in the changing scene that we don't notice that we've slipped out of the present moment.

It's important to recognize that all unhappiness exists in time. Another way to understand this is that time is born when your true self has been sacrificed for your self-image. We've already touched on self-image and its false promises. Time, being the movement of thought, uses your self-image or ego as your internal reference point. If you look closely at what is happening in your mind, what do you see?

You are constantly evaluating every experience.
You are comparing yourself to something that seems
    better or worse.

You are rejecting some things and choosing others.
You are building up a story.

None of these activities is actually necessary. They merely accumulate reasons to be happy or unhappy. One way to do that is to compare your situation with someone else's. But as you build your story and look around to see if it is better or worse than your neighbor's, what's happening? You've moved away from the natural state of happiness that exists in the now. Experience is. You don't have to use it to build up a story. The ego loves melodrama, so it seizes upon every experience to construct a never-ending tale about how your life is going. The tale can be good or bad, dramatic or boring, self-centered or relatively selfless. But what if you had no story? Your life would be much simpler and more natural. You would have no self-image to defend. You would have no fear of tomorrow because with nothing at stake about how your story is going, you could accept any experience and let it go. In that state, both freedom and bliss reside.

One of my favorite sayings is that being here is enough. When people hear this, particularly successful people whose lives are full of projects and accomplishments, they look confused. To them, "being here" sounds passive and empty.

Yet think about it. As they pursue lives that are so full of activity and goals, most people are not fulfilling their being. Quite the opposite. They are running away from a deep-seated fear that life is empty unless you constantly fill it up.

One time I saw a great spiritual teacher being confronted by a person in deep distress. This person faced the prospect of losing all his money and his job. He felt desperate, and he wanted to hear what a wise man would tell him. After he recited his tale of woe, the great teacher replied with a simple answer: "Souls don't break. They bounce."

Fear has been lying to us, as is so often the case. If you could allow your mind to stop participating in the endless pursuit of goals, time would stop. You would experience your being. At that moment, you would realize that "being here" is your rock, your foundation. The quality of being leads to the quality of consciousness. The quality of your consciousness determines the quality of your life. We all owe our existence to the fact that existence isn't empty.

The ego drives you to identify with the changing world. It keeps your focus on everything but your being. Think of all the things you have a stake in—home, family, career, money, possessions, status, religion, politics, and world affairs. They are all ego creations. They are housed in the complex edifice of time. When you break through the barrier of the ego, you also break through the barrier of time.

The eternal now is the junction point between the unmanifest, invisible world of spirit and the manifest, visible world that you accept as real. Few people know that they live in both of these realities. Still less do they know that the unmanifest, invisible world is their primary reality. Compared to it, the visible world is a playhouse of shadows. So when you focus on the present moment, you are actually looking through a window to the unbounded timeless reality from which the entire universe arises and to which it subsides.

The outer world arises in every moment of now. Its next birth is never the same as the one that came before. Constant change is the rule; constant transformation upholds every process, including the process of life. So your true self can be defined as a still point surrounded by transformation. If you allow yourself to be absorbed in this still point, you will be changeless in the midst of change.

You need to learn to separate the moment from the situation. They aren't the same. The situation surrounds the present moment. It can be unpleasant and painful or the opposite. But the situation, whatever it is, arises and subsides. It will pass. The eternal now, which is always present, will remain. People talk about having so much pain that it is inescapable. But all such pain is born of thought, and is therefore changeable. I have seen patients with severe chronic pain, and when a few of them were able to separate their situation from the present moment, all but miraculously their pain disappeared. They had transcended a pain born in time. This taught me that even the most extreme situations can be transcended.

In order to transcend your situation, you must cultivate a new style of awareness, where you have your attention on what is, and you see the fullness in every moment. Most people are not actually focusing on what is. They are overshadowing the experience of what is with what could be or what was. The past and future dominate their attention. When you embrace what is with your whole attention, you will be immersed in the fullness of the now.

So how do we cultivate this new form of attention? Primarily through mindfulness. *Mindfulness* means "paying attention," but in a special way that your mind isn't used to. At any given moment your mind is paying attention to things that have nothing to do with the present moment. The list of possibilities is long.

Your mind may be feeling distracted and stressed.

It may be daydreaming, engaging in fantasy.

It may be worrying.

It may be reliving old memories.

It may be making future plans.

It may be planning ways to take control of the situation.

It may be defending its cherished beliefs.

It is almost certainly telling you a very familiar story.

What's useful about this list is that it tells you in simple terms what mindfulness is not. Instead of struggling to be mindful, it's easier to stop doing the opposite. When you notice that your mind is engaging in any activity that pulls you out of the present moment, simply stop. Don't evaluate or analyze. Don't accuse yourself of something wrong. By simply observing what's going on and letting it come to a stop, you have entered the domain of mindfulness.

Many people have never experienced their minds at rest. Reading through the list above, they would say, "But that's what my mind is for. That's who I am." No, you do not exist to support the activity of the mind. The mind exists to support you. One of the best ways it can do so is by allowing you to experience reality, not the fluctuating reality of the material world but the changeless reality untouched by time.

Other people are able to experience a few moments of restfulness in their minds, perhaps by focusing or meditating on their breath, or on a mantra, but almost immediately the old restless mind activity returns. What then? Move into the mode of simple attention. There are many areas of life to be mindful of besides the buzzing activity of the mind. You can be mindful of your emotions, your breath, or the sensations in your body. You can be aware of the sounds in your surroundings. The way you move your body—sitting, walking, eating, or any other activity—can be the object of your mindfulness.

It's important not to try or use effort. Anything you draw your attention to will bring you into the present moment, giving you the experience of *presence*. When you are in the proximity of a holy person, for example, you experience divinity that is actually rooted in something much simpler: it comes from being present. Being present is enough to bestow calm and a subtle feeling of safety, love, and joy. We often miss this experience in our own lives, because as soon as we have a thought or sensation, we start to evaluate and analyze it. When we do so the present disappears, and takes presence with it.

Being present and experiencing presence are the same, and neither one requires effort. You cannot work to be present. You just are. If you practice mindfulness, this quality of joyful presence will begin to be with you all the time. If you find yourself getting distracted, just noticing that you are distracted will bring you back to the present. The kind of mindfulness I am talking about has nothing to do with emptiness, or checking out. It doesn't require concentration or intensity. It is the most relaxed and natural state because nothing is more relaxed than your self. You can slip into it simply by noticing each distracting activity and letting it go. "Easy come, easy go" actually has a deep spiritual meaning. What comes and goes isn't the real you. The real you is the bliss that exists beyond time.

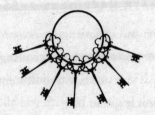

To Activate the *Fifth Key*
in Everyday Life, I Promise Myself
to Do the Following:

1. I will embrace what is, and not impose upon it what was or what could be. What is brings me into the present moment. It sheds worry and anticipation. By focusing only on what is before me, I am in a new mind-set that is far more relaxed and accepting. I am allowing my own being to be present. In this way I experience the fullness of divine presence.

2. I will catch myself whenever I am distracted. I am not the restless activity of the mind. I am not the story my mind is constantly telling me. I am not my memories, or my dreams of the future. I am the point of stillness, now and evermore. As soon as I stop being distracted, I am being mindful. Now I can pay attention to the present moment and the fullness it contains.

3. I will separate the present moment from the present situation. Every situation rises and subsides. Things change, but I remain. If a stressful situation continues, I will find a quiet place to gather myself. If that isn't possible, I promise to walk away at the first opportunity. This is the practical value of mindfulness. It reminds me that my primary aim in life is to be present with my true self. Only then can I appreciate what is.

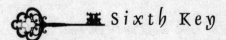 Sixth Key

SEE THE WORLD IN YOURSELF

When you see the world in yourself, there
are no more outward obstacles to happiness.
The inner and outer worlds are mirrors of
each other. They change according to your level
of consciousness. If you are vibrating at the
level of fear, your inner world of thoughts and
emotions and your outer world of events and
relationships will reflect that. Similarly, if
your consciousness vibrates at the level of love,
then love will be present in both your inner
and outer worlds. A flow of happiness and
abundance will manifest when you have
reached the deepest level of yourself.

In oneself lies the whole world, and if you know
how to look and learn, the door is there and the
key is in your hand.

—J. Krishnamurti

I am the light that makes experience possible.
I am the reality which is hidden in all beings.

—Yoga Vasishtha

Know that the outer world reflects your inner reality. It has no other option. As we saw, you live in two domains at the same time, and the unmanifest, invisible domain is primary. Whatever occurs at the deepest level of the unmanifest must come into being as an outer event, situation, challenge, crisis, or opportunity. The unmanifest is where the script of your life is written.

If that is so, naturally you would want to write a script that includes happiness, joy, and love. So why is it so rare for life to bring us those things? Without understanding deeper levels of consciousness, you will not be able to take advantage of them. Several conditions must be accepted by you as true:

Consciousness exists everywhere.
It is infinitely flexible.
Reality changes in different states of consciousness.

We are used to thinking that the opposite of these statements is true. We limit consciousness to the brain, we assume that a person's level of awareness is fixed, and we believe that reality is essentially the same for everyone. The irony is that the universe, being a conscious entity, reflects those very beliefs. To truly unite your inner and outer worlds, a shift is needed in your belief system.

Your true identity is neither the inner nor the outer world. You are the creator of both. The same source that creates thoughts, feelings, memories, emotions, and all subjective experience simultaneously creates the objective world that matches your subjective state. If you don't like what is happening around you, don't try to "fix it." That would be like polishing the mirror hoping to change the reflection you see in it. In order to change what you see, there has to be a new message coming from the source.

Our current belief system, which insists that something must be tangible and concrete to be real, traps consciousness inside the brain. This is far too limiting. There is a ground state beyond space and time that conceives, governs, and creates all the events that occur in space-time. Imagine that before you have a thought or before an event takes place in the world, it begins as a seed in the ground state. The seed vibrates to life, moving from the subtlest level of nature to the grossest level, where the five senses can detect it. Quantum physics completely agrees with this idea. It even accepts that thoughts "in here" must come from the ground state, just like electrons and photons "out there." The difference is that the world's wisdom traditions link the two. They give primary value to awareness while physics gives primary value to inert matter, although this is beginning to change.

Suppose you don't like a situation in your life. You perceive that there is an outside circumstance or relationship that is at fault. Merely turning to positive thinking isn't going to make a difference. You can think as positively as you like about your troubles, but this is a superficial mood; it doesn't go to the source. In fact, to artificially manipulate your thoughts, even in a positive direction, can increase stress and worsen the situation. The solution is to change both inner and outer reality simultaneously. Consciousness permeates everything. It functions to create change at four fundamental levels: being, feeling, thinking, and doing.

The highest level of consciousness is *pure being*. We see this in the innocence of a child; there is spontaneity, wonder, joy, and playfulness. When you are established at this level of consciousness, your thoughts and actions will reflect these qualities. Pure being has no qualities we can label, but that doesn't mean it is empty. In the stillness and silence of being, you contact the ground state that physicists talk about. The poet William Blake called this the state of organized innocence, which means that innocence has gained the power to organize all of life. If you live from the level of pure being, in practice you have mastered creation. The laws of Nature come to your aid whenever you call on them using the power of intention.

Since consciousness transcends personal identity, living from the level of pure being arouses the deepest values of life. Eastern wisdom traditions list four of these values that are most harmonious to human existence. These constitute the highest level of *feeling*:

1. Loving kindness
2. Compassion
3. Joy at the success of others
4. Equanimity, peace

We might call these qualities of the heart, which exist on the feeling level when a person achieves the highest level of thought. Thought gains its integrity from feelings. In your mind you can think all kinds of charitable, kind, peaceful thoughts, but your whole being isn't really behind them. They exist as empty ideas so the outer world can still bring you severely unloving reflections. But if your thoughts are based on genuine feelings that spring from your deepest being, then the outcome of this process—the actions you take in the world—will bring fulfillment.

When people complain that life is unfair, what they are really saying is that there is a mismatch between inner events (hopes, wishes, expectations, ambitions, goals) and the response of the outer world. In our society we constantly reinforce the idea that we should follow our dreams, but what about the millions of people whose dreams have faded? In some way the chain that leads from being to feeling to thinking and then to doing has been broken.

Restoring the sequence isn't difficult, but you must move things in the right direction. Pure being leads to the highest level of feeling, and the highest level of feeling creates the highest level of thinking and doing. Now we see the solution to being a loving person in an unloving world. You don't struggle to be loving; you don't oppose those who are unloving. Instead, you establish yourself in pure being, which is loving by nature, and then inner and outer reality cannot help but reflect who you are.

This picture of reality streaming from one source creates a radical transformation at every level. Take thinking. As we saw, most of the time the mind is occupied with distractions, unable to focus on the present moment. Habits of worrying, fretting, planning, and dwelling in fantasy are by-products of disconnection from pure being. The highest level of thinking is a constant flow of creativity from the source that is accompanied by feelings of joy and compassion. The final result is doing. No one has to be told what it's like to act out of conflict, stress, anxiety, indecision, and doubt. We know that all of these are mental obstacles to right action. The highest level of doing is completely clear. Since it comes from a level beyond personality, such action reaches beyond personal benefit. It benefits everything around you, beginning with your family and extending to the entire world. If you want to help humanity, the surest way is to act while you're established in pure being.

It's important to realize that the mechanics of consciousness aren't theoretical or abstract. In daily life you can readily observe that when you move away from your core experience of happiness, both the outer world and the inner world are in a disturbed state. This is a signal that you have disconnected yourself from your true self. Before you react by trying to manipulate either your thoughts or the situation, step back and reconnect to being. You know how to be mindful. It involves taking your attention away from the situation and going back to the self. Is this a cure-all for every bad circumstance in life? No, but the reasons why mindfulness might fall short tell us a great deal:

> If mindfulness is superficial, it has less influence; your
>   mind must be able to reach a deeper level.
> Inner resistance, past traumas, and rigid beliefs block
>   the flow of consciousness. When consciousness is blocked,
>   it loses its power.

Almost all the work done on the spiritual path consists of two things: clearing away obstacles, and reaching a deeper level of awareness. In these ways you open a connection to your true self and you remove the ego's resistance. Yet even at the beginning of the path, being mindful of your role as the witness is very effective. When you achieve this state, you are grounded, alert, flexible, and ready to act from the highest level. Shifting to the witness is a subtle action. It requires that you "just stop."

If that feels too difficult—as it does to many people, because they have never taken time to simply be with themselves—then just move to observing your breath. If you observe your breath without manipulating it, it will start to slow down. The breath leads the body. It is the subtlest physical response, mirroring the movement of consciousness. You cannot hide your true feelings and reactions from your breathing. As you continue to observe your breath, you will feel calm and centered. Your thoughts will settle down, and the external stress will not seem so threatening. You are actually changing your vibration at the level of being.

With a little experience of what it is like to be still, you will be able to access the highest level of feeling. This can be done by recalling an experience of love. Let yourself be immersed in what it was like to be in love or feel deeply loved. Once you have a clear connection to this feeling, ask for guidance from your deepest awareness. It will respond either with a creative insight or a meaningful understanding. Quite often this connection arises in the form of a coincidence or unexpected turn of events. Why is that? Because we are so used to following the biased guidance of the ego, whose agenda includes payback, ambition, insecurity, and self-importance, that the true self must communicate through surprising or unexpected events. But no matter what route they take, messages from your deepest awareness are being sent all the time.

Now you can take action from the highest level, knowing that the consequences of your action benefit everyone in the situation. The benefit may be obvious or subtle, immediate or delayed. It isn't up to you to manipulate things so everyone comes away happy. Your obligation is only to execute the sequential unfolding of consciousness at its highest levels: being, feeling, thinking, and doing. The New Testament uses an enigmatic phrase for this: being in the world but not of it. Now we have clarified what these words mean. You render everything around you—people, circumstances, situations and their stresses—almost irrelevant. You still participate in that world, but you are rooted in the deeper reality from which it springs. Living from your source unites the inner and outer world. It transcends both and gives your thoughts the force of Nature itself.

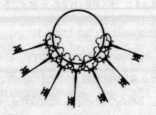

To Activate the *Sixth Key* in Everyday Life, I Promise Myself to Do the Following:

1. I will learn to step into the domain of being. Today I will be mindful; I will meditate; I will repair the connection to my true self. Only by experiencing pure being can I find a solid foundation for everything I feel, think, and do.

2. No matter how uncomfortable or unpleasant an experience may be today, I will meet it with highest consciousness. I will connect with my being, find the highest feeling of love within myself, and let my deepest consciousness deliver the action I should take.

3. When I find myself reacting with anger or opposition to any person or circumstance, I will realize that I am only struggling with myself. Putting up resistance is a response created by old hurts. When I relinquish this anger, I will be healing myself and cooperating with the flow of the universe.

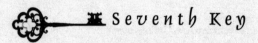 Seventh Key

LIVE FOR ENLIGHTENMENT

To seek enlightenment is to seek your true self.
Enlightenment is the most aware state of
existence and also the most natural, because it
is where you came from. Your home is a place
of profound love, peace, and joy. When you
return there, you will experience yourself
as one with God. At that moment you will
realize that your desire for happiness was only
the beginning. Your deepest desire was for the
freedom that comes with complete awakening.

I look into your eyes and see the whole
universe—born and not yet born.

—*Rumi*

A human being is a creature who has received
the order to become God.

—*St. Basil*

Being fulfilled means going beyond everyday experience. At a deeper level human beings have always longed for ecstasy, a feeling of euphoria, joy, peace, and love. Addiction to drugs and alcohol is evidence of our society's starvation and longing for real ecstasy. Everyday happiness gives us only a taste, leaving behind a hunger for more. Happiness, then, is the beginning of a journey that reaches for higher fulfillment.

Many people have accidentally experienced the most intense happiness, often called a peak experience. These experiences may have occurred in intimate moments in Nature, in dance and music, in play, or in lovemaking. What sets a peak experience apart is not its intensity but its meaning—it feels as if a much greater, freer, more expansive reality has been revealed. Everyone who has had a peak experience tries to recapture it. Most are disappointed, because a moment of higher awareness isn't the same as attaining higher awareness. What is needed is a path to transformation guided by a vision of the possibilities that the first taste inspires.

In the world's wisdom traditions, the search for ecstasy is completely natural. Ecstasy is your original energy state. To return to it is to return home and make it your permanent abode. There are many names for this goal: redemption, salvation, transcendence, and enlightenment. There are as many paths as there are faiths and spiritual teachers. But in the end a single truth is being espoused: The human soul longs to return to the place where ecstasy abides. There, union can be found with the mystery of God.

Is it possible to expand your consciousness until it merges with God's consciousness? The answer offered by wisdom traditions is yes, but for the individual, the only proof lies in experiencing that union. A life decision is required. Flashes of intense happiness, even a moment of ecstasy, can happen spontaneously—the clouds clear and suddenly you see the sun. But seeking enlightenment implies a shift that you make of your own free will. Instead of pursuing happiness, you pursue bliss. The problem for most people is that such a shift seems extreme, alien, and perhaps threatening. This is understandable. As wisdom traditions declined, a false belief sprang up about enlightenment. It became identified with renunciation, sacrifice, poverty, and solitude.

None of that is true. How could discovering your true

self possibly be a form of sacrifice? But your ego benefits from this misperception by making you feel that there is no other self but the one it has shown you. It is up to you to discover the truth. When you become mindful, you begin to witness what is happening in and around you. The witness sees what the ego tries to hide, that daily life is not fulfilling when your deepest desire has been blocked.

In the previous chapters we explored different ways to make the necessary shift. Now let's look farther ahead on the journey. You can gain a glimpse of enlightenment with a simple exercise. Close your eyes and imagine a beautiful sunset over the ocean. See the colors as vividly as possible; catch the shining glint of the sun off the water. Now open your eyes. Did you see the sunset? That picture was not in your brain. If we looked inside your brain, we would find electrochemical reactions coursing through synaptic networks. There are no images inside the brain that match what our eyes see. There isn't the slightest glimmer of light inside the visual cortex. But when you close your eyes and imagine a sunset, you don't experience electrochemical reactions. Where, then, is the picture of the sunset you saw? It exists not in your brain but in consciousness. The same holds true if you try to imagine anything with your five senses—the smell of a rose, the sound of a newborn baby crying, the soft texture of velvet, or a full-blown kiss on the lips. There are no sights or sounds or tastes or smells in your brain, only a dark silence flickering with faint electrical impulses and chemical exchanges. Every sensation exists in consciousness alone.

Now extend this awareness to your body. You experience your body as a series of sensations—the weight of your limbs, the in and out of your breathing, the thumping rhythm of your heart when you run. But, once again, none of these sensations can be found in your brain, even with advanced imaging like CAT scans and functional MRIs. Only electrochemical signals register on these scans. Therefore, your body also exists in your consciousness. There is nowhere else to experience it.

Look at the world around you. Everything about its color, sound, taste, and smell seems totally real, but where is this world located? If you pick up a rock lying in the sun, your past conditioning leads you to say, "If this rock feels heavy and warm, it's real." But if your body, which also feels heavy and warm, exists only in consciousness, so does a rock. Anything you can possibly experience, extending out to the farthest reaches of the cosmos, exists in your consciousness. To find your home, you must find where this consciousness resides.

Now ask the ultimate question: Where do *you* exist? If the world cannot be found inside your brain, the same is even more true for you, because no MRI has ever found a part of the brain that lights up when you experience yourself. Yet you know you have a self. To find it, you must think outside the brain, in fact outside time and space. You are pure consciousness, which has no location in time and space. Think of how television works. When you watch TV, you can locate the screen in your living room. That picture only exists because of signals from the transmitter. Those signals are everywhere. Amazing as it may seem, even though you can locate your body in time and space, your consciousness is everywhere, which means that you are, too. The only reason your brain lights up is because consciousness causes it to.

Beginning with a simple exercise, like imagining a sunset over the ocean, we arrive at an astounding truth: You are holding the world together simply by observing it. The witness turns a formless swirl of photons into everything we see, hear, touch, taste, and smell. You don't have to do anything to accomplish this. Subtle intention is enough. You want to see a sunset, and you do. There's no need to instruct the brain how to build the image out of electrochemical impulses. Likewise, if you want to walk down the street, you don't have to instruct your muscles how to fire and your cardiovascular system how to bring blood to the muscles. Simply by having a wordless intention, all the right connections are made.

You hold the world together at a very subtle level, the source of creation known as God. Together, you and God produce reality, and neither of you has to struggle to do it. To be enlightened is to be attuned to this simple fact. As the upholder of creation, your role is to be, nothing else. In that realization life becomes effortless. All stress, strain, worry, anxiety, and uncertainty drop away. The secret of unbounded bliss has been revealed.

Now you know your goal and the path that will take you there. How can you tell when you are making progress on the path? By referring every day to the following indicators:

1. Your life flows with effortless spontaneity.
2. Love is becoming the motivating factor in your life.
3. You are discovering hidden sources of creativity and imagination.
4. You are accepting higher guidance into your life.
5. Your choices benefit you and all those around you.

Yet we could reduce all these indications to one: You are expanding the experience of happiness wherever you go.

As a boy in India I was given very simple lessons about spirituality. One of them was that enlightenment is like running back into the arms of your mother. Every child can relate to that sensation. It still holds true when you are an adult, contemplating what the spiritual path means. The journey is a progressive expansion from ordinary waking consciousness, with all its fear and isolation, to soul consciousness, which is safe, warm, and welcoming.

Having run into the arms of your soul, you are home. You no longer identify with ego boundaries. You find that you are not in the world; the world is in you. Everything to be said about consciousness comes down to this. Because the journey never ends, there is more to gain. Simply by being aware of your true self, you will progress naturally and easily to cosmic consciousness, which is the same as being fully awake twenty-four hours a day even when your body and brain are sleeping. Next you will expand to divine consciousness, or God consciousness, in which everything is made of light. Divine presence emanates from every object, every experience, and every thought. (This stage is sometimes known as wearing golden spectacles, because a radiant light fills your awareness.)

Finally, you will arrive at unity consciousness, where all divisions and separations end. Every moment is part of eternity. Every experience is shared with the cosmos. Unity consciousness was described by William Blake when he wrote, "To see a world in a grain of sand, And a heaven in a wild flower, Hold infinity in the palm of your hand, And eternity in an hour."

With all of this stretching before you, consider where you are today. If you are serious about following your path, the possibility for happiness is infinitely expanded. You will be heading for nothing less than enlightenment. You shouldn't think of enlightenment as it is often portrayed, as a mystical state. In reality consciousness expands naturally. The state of bliss is your birthright. When you attain higher consciousness in any form, through devotion, compassion, service, or knowledge of the self, you will be on the same journey that we have been taking since the first page of this book—and the first day of our lives. If consciousness is your true home, so is enlightenment your true destination.

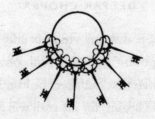

TO ACTIVATE THE *Seventh* Key
IN EVERYDAY LIFE, I PROMISE MYSELF
TO DO THE FOLLOWING:

1. I will remember that ecstasy is my primordial energy state. It is my source. I can return to it anytime I want. What is needed is a shift in attention away from my ego's desires to the deeper desire in me, which is to find my true self.

2. I will see my thoughts, my body, and my surroundings as a single process. This process occurs in consciousness. There are no divisions in reality. Feeling separate, helpless, or alone is an indication that I have lost contact with the process. When I am part of the flow of life, all things are different aspects of one thing: the unfolding of myself.

3. I will keep alive my vision of life, a journey from waking consciousness to soul consciousness, where full awareness can never be lost. From that point, real life begins, for my path will take me to cosmic consciousness, divine consciousness, and finally to unity consciousness. Whenever I am distracted by the outside world and its constant demands, I will remember my vision and keep to my path. Enlightenment is my destination. When I arrive, I will be home at last.

Happiness Will Heal the World

An old way of being happy has brought the world to the brink of peril. A new way of being happy can save it. These are drastic statements, but if they are true, a profound change can occur, and its effect will only be positive. All the problems we see around us are the result of individuals making choices. No matter how huge a challenge may be, from global warming to nuclear arms, from AIDS to overpopulation, the seed of the problem was a decision to act in a certain way. When the decision was being made, the person making it tried to create more happiness or to avoid unhappiness. The question is how to make choices that lead to happiness without leading to unforeseen disaster.

That cannot be done when happiness is defined the old way, even though the old way felt safe. Owning a car and driving it to work makes most people happier than walking. Having a child makes married couples happy. Raking leaves in the fall and burning them in a pile was the mark of a responsible citizen in years past. Yet in the long run these simple actions resulted in global problems. Happiness can be blamed even for self-destructive behavior. During the Cold War the buildup of nuclear arms began as a way to keep us safe, for example, yet very soon the United States and the Soviet Union had achieved mutually assured destruction— that is, pushing a button to launch the first missile would set off a chain of events that would annihilate both nations.

Even before global warming and the arms race, people made choices every day in pursuit of happiness that didn't actually lead to happiness. The old way of being happy carried certain beliefs and conditions that ensured unhappy results:

> *Each person is alone and must struggle to fulfill*
> *his desires.*
> *The basic state of Nature is one of lack. There are not*
> *enough of the good things in life to go around.*
> *The environment is hostile and therefore to survive*
> *means a life of struggle.*
> *It is desirable to accumulate material goods without end.*
> *Rich equals fulfilled.*
> *If you don't look after yourself, no one will.*
> *Making yourself happy today is more important than*
> *thinking about tomorrow.*

Countless people pursue happiness without questioning these beliefs, but there will be no happiness for the world until we break their spell. Let me relate a moment in my own life that helped me to break it. I had taken my six-year-old granddaughter to the beach and watched her as she waded in the shallow water. She came to me to be dried off, and as I leaned over her, I smelled the salty smell of the sea in her hair. When I took her home, she said good-bye and I kissed her on the cheek, which still tasted salty from her splashing in the sea.

Suddenly I realized, "Here is the oneness of life." The salt in the sea is the same salt that runs through every living thing. Simply smelling the sea brings a cloud of salt molecules into your body, and when you kiss someone on the cheek, the sense of taste brings more molecules from their body to yours. Nothing goes unshared. When you smell cigarette smoke from someone, you are inhaling particles of polluted air that were in someone's lungs. Every moment we inhale viruses that incubated in someone else's cells—these harmful microorganisms represent a worldwide circulation of DNA from one life form to another. In the poem "Song of Myself," Walt Whitman said, "Every atom belonging to you as well belongs to me."

You are inescapably woven into the web of life. Think of a tree in tropical Africa, a squirrel in Siberia, a camel in Saudi Arabia, a Chinese peasant harvesting rice, or a taxi driver zooming through the smog-filled streets of Calcutta. You have raw material inside your tissues that was circulating in those bodies less than twenty days ago. Your body is not your own. It never was. The mathematics of radioactive decay reveals that each of us has at least a million atoms in our bodies that were once in the body of Christ, Buddha, Genghis Khan, or any other historical figure. In just the last three weeks a quadrillion atoms (10 followed by 15 zeros) have passed through your body that were previously circulating through every living species on this planet.

This sharing extends to subtler levels of existence, too. Each thought circulates around the planet thanks to the Internet, entering other nervous systems and being absorbed by them. Communications devices run on electricity, so once again we are part of one energy field and one information field. Likewise, our emotions are not confined to us. Anxiety over the economic meltdown enters every house in the world, producing shared responses among billions of people. When you feel your blood pressure rise, your heart race, and your skin grow cold, the same anxious reactions are affecting everyone who shares your extended emotions.

I've articulated this insight many times in many ways, but at that moment, watching my granddaughter get out of the car and run back into the house, the impact was undeniable. It was instantly clear that I couldn't possibly hope to be happy in isolation, much less hope to be enlightened. I can take refuge in the illusion that "I" am separate, that "I" can compete against "you" to get what I want, with one of us winning while the other loses out. But this refuge is the most dangerous place anyone could live. The sense of separation causes us to make choices that come back to haunt us. All because salt molecules are drifting from the sea to a human body, and then another and another, without end.

I try to remind myself often of a quote from the English physicist and astronomer Sir James Jeans: "In the deeper reality . . . we may all be members of one body." This is the first principle of the new happiness outlined in this book. It breaks the spell of separation; it makes possible the healing of the world at a time of great insecurity and crisis.

The second principle is that we all exist inside one another, because the air, food, and water that we take in and expel are in constant circulation.

The third principle is that this constant circulation is one process. Nature is behaving as a whole, leaving not a single atom outside the tapestry.

If these principles are true, a shift in awareness is the only way that happiness today can be attained without unhappiness coming along in the future. Currently, the happiness that people experience depends on someone else being unhappy (through poverty, exploitation, war, crime, and class division), or else on blinding ourselves to how insecure today's happiness actually is when tomorrow brings a change.

We all have a global stake in creating happiness that is true and enduring. For many, the phrase "happiness will heal the world" sounds too far-fetched and wishful. And it's true that a nice feeling or a sense of personal contentment doesn't heal the world, far from it. But at a basic level, happy people wouldn't choose to develop chemical weapons, start terrorist movements, commit acts of torture, and start wars. If even a small group of people found their true selves and thereby attained the happiness that can never be taken away, they would live at a deep level of awareness. From that level, the influence radiated out into their surroundings would be profound.

They would add an element to the world's consciousness best described as "coherence." (In an age of faith, we might call this saintliness, purity, or the peace that passes understanding.) This is everyone's ground state, because coherence is natural; no cell in your body could remain alive for three seconds if life wasn't systematic, organized, balanced, and interconnected. At the level of awareness, to be coherent in yourself means that you are:

At peace
Nonviolent
Awake and aware
Fearless
Without conflict and illusions
Resilient
Independent, free of outside influences

These shouldn't be rare qualities. But they are when people grow unhappy, and their incoherence radiates out into the surroundings. Individual incoherence advances a state of chaos, confusion, and conflict. From that state, which all of us have known in our personal lives, the unhappy problems of the world follow as naturally as night follows day. When asked how to prevent war, J. Krishnamurti uttered something profound. He said, "Change yourself. Your own anger and violence are the cause of all wars."

The world has let incoherence spread like a pandemic. Now we must test whether coherence can have the opposite effect, bringing an end to chaos, conflict, and confusion on a global scale.

It was always true that we were dependent on one another for our emotional and physical well-being. A harsh word from someone else can cause physical havoc in your body. A loving word can turn havoc into harmony. Emotions such as love, compassion, empathy, and joy bring the body back to a state of balance known as homeostasis: self-repair mechanisms are triggered; a biological healing response is the result. If you are in such a state of well-being and I am around you, I will be affected in the same way. My physiology will mirror yours.

The underlying truth seems undeniable: My happiness can heal someone else just the way it heals me. The most important contribution I can make to the healing of our planet is therefore to be happy. By spreading that happiness wherever I go, I create a healing response. It's crucial to realize that this doesn't require doing anything special—you don't have to focus on acts of loving kindness, although if they are spontaneous expressions of your happiness, that's wonderful. It is not by saying or doing that we create the most profound change around us. As Ralph Waldo Emerson once said, "Who you are is shouting so loudly that I can't hear what you're saying." The more intense your state of happiness, the greater its healing effect.

The healing influence of happiness travels literally at the speed of light. Like a single inspiring thought that goes on the Internet and reaches millions of people in a matter of hours, one person's happiness is unbounded. It multiplies exponentially like a benign infection, creating greater order in place of disorder, greater unity in place of separation. So rather than clinging to a limited identity, see yourself on a world scale. If you are on the path to unity consciousness, it's a small step to imagine happiness on a world scale, as part of humanity's extended body, mind, and spirit. A matrix binds us together that is beyond any energy field or information field. It's a spiritual field. This is the manifestation of what religions call the mind of God.

Now the vision is complete. As the ancient philosopher Plotinus said, "Our concern is not merely to be sinless, but to be God." The happiest existence anyone can imagine is to live in the mind of God, a mind made fully human, which was God's intention all along. Everything we fear in the world and want to change can be transformed through happiness, the simplest desire we have, and also the most profound.

Acknowledgments

My deep appreciation goes to the dedicated people who made this book possible. At the Chopra Center, Carolyn, Felicia, and Lindsay support me through their tireless work. My longtime editor, Peter Guzzardi, has become an alter ego whose judgment I can always rely upon. Many thanks to Julia Pastore and Tara Gilbride at Harmony Books. Finally, a special thanks to Shaye Areheart, who has championed my books through good times and bad in the publishing industry. Your trust warms my heart and helps make everything worthwhile.

Also available from Rider

You Are the Universe
Discovering Your Cosmic Self and Why It Matters

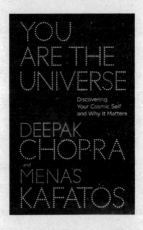

Bestselling author Deepak Chopra joins forces with
leading physicist Menas Kafatos to explore nine of the
biggest and most baffling questions about science and the
nature of reality. Their answers will present a bold new
understanding of who we are and how we can reach our
greatest potential.

ISBN: 9781846045301

Order direct from www.penguin.co.uk

Also available from Rider

Radical Beauty

How to transform yourself from the inside out

Deepak Chopra and Kimberly Snyder offer an exciting and practical programme to help transform you from the inside out. Through six pillars of healthy living that focus on such topics as internal and external nourishment, sleep, living naturally, avoiding excessive stress, and better understanding the relationship between emotions and inflammatory foods, they offer 'radical routines' and 'radical foods' that will have the best impact on your body and mind.

ISBN: 9781846045240

Order direct from www.penguin.co.uk

Also available from Rider

Super Genes
The hidden key to total well-being

DEEPAK
CHOPRA

RUDOLPH
E. TANZI

Super Genes includes meditation and breathing practical
exercises, as well as information on how to manage risk
factors for disease. Combining scientific research with
insights from ancient traditions, Chopra and Tanzi show
how we need not be at the mercy of our genetic inheri-
tance. Instead, they argue, we have the power to rewire our
super genes for health and happiness.

ISBN: 9781846045035

Order direct from www.penguin.co.uk

Also available from Rider

Ageless Body, Timeless Mind
A Practical Alternative To Growing Old

Ageless Body, Timeless Mind goes beyond ancient mind/body wisdom and current anti-aging research to show you do not have to grow old. Deepak Chopra bases his theories on the ancient Indian science of Ayurveda, according to which, optimum health is about achieving balance physically, emotionally and psychologically, and demonstrates that, contrary to our traditional beliefs about aging, we can use our innate capacity for balance to direct the way our bodies metabolize time and achieve our unbounded potential.

ISBN: 9781846041044

Order direct from www.penguin.co.uk